T0374046

Invitation

Love Letters 101

Ivan G. Hall

AuthorHouse™
1663 Liberty Drive
Bloomington, IN 47403
www.authorhouse.com
Phone: 1-800-839-8640

© 2011 Ivan G. Hall. All rights reserved.

No part of this book may be reproduced, stored in a retrieval system,
or transmitted by any means without the written permission of the author.

First published by AuthorHouse   1/28/2011

ISBN: 978-1-4567-3379-7 (sc)

Library of Congress Control Number: 2011901354

Printed in the United States of America

Any people depicted in stock imagery provided by Thinkstock are models,
and such images are being used for illustrative purposes only.
Certain stock imagery © Thinkstock.

This book is printed on acid-free paper.

Because of the dynamic nature of the Internet, any web addresses or links contained in this book may have changed
since publication and may no longer be valid. The views expressed in this work are solely those of the author and do not
necessarily reflect the views of the publisher, and the publisher hereby disclaims any responsibility for them.

Preface

With all the elements that work against us coming together as a people, communication should be the one thing that we use properly. It's almost as if expressions of true love have become a lost art. With this project it is my sincere hope that the advancement of passion between men and women is realized in the most intimate way. Our LORD JESUS issued an eleventh commandment, (John 13:34, 14:12), that we should love one another as he loved us. I pray that we can begin with two people at a time to improve our relationships, our families and our lives with just a few expressions of love. If you find it hard to communicate the simple words "I love you", perhaps this project can help.

Dedication

I would like to dedicate this collection to the memory of my mother and father, William and Aurelia Hall who set an example of real love and always stressed proper education along with the ability to express ones self. They were the best parents a child could have, also to my neighborhood, (my village), Oaklawn Park in Charlotte N.C. Growing up with a host of friends and Adults who all treat you like family shaped the values and the love that exist in my heart today. Thank you.

To Denise, this project would not exist without your love. Thank you so very much for being my muse. You are the "Gorgeous One", the one that makes my dreams come true. The one and only one, and no one else could ever do.

Acknowledgements

First and foremost I want to thank my lord JESUS CHRIST, my mighty GOD JEHOVAH, and the HOLY SPIRIT without whom I simply would not be. All praises and glory to my LORD.

I want to thank Sameemah Wilborn, the entire Pinckney family for making me one of their own, Oswald Neal for being a life long friend and a brother, Wiley Thompson and Cameron Scott. A very special thanks to Wendell G. Chaplin and Diana R. Jones for their faith in me and this project and their contribution of love and guidance, also to the Hennigan family for just being so good to me and giving me a very special love.

There are times when we are fortunate and blessed enough to experience angels in our lives. They can take human form and be there in the most adverse situations to simply do the work of GOD and give us the most incredible insight and gifts from above. My good friends, Mark Peskir and George Simmons are two such angels that have made a big difference in my life. Thank you so much.

I want to give a very special thanks to Dr. Spurgeon Webber III for his ongoing support and friendship. Real friends are so hard to find and you are one of the best.

There is a very special element in this project that gives it a dimension all its own. I would like to thank my good friend Mr. Clarence Leak Sr. for his contribution of photography to this book. You have an amazing eye for color, and a depth perception that is unmatched as well as the true spirit of an artist. I am proud to call you my friend.

Contents

x

Invitation

You are cordially invited to a very special event, true love for the rest of your life. The time begins now and it happens everywhere you are. There is no RSVP necessary. Dress code is optional. The menu is yet to be determined, but you know when you're with me you will eat very well. All you will need is a willing heart, a loving soul and a little faith. Custom designed just for you, this love has some incredible features and benefits. All the love you can stand, a friendship that is unmatched, 24 hour a day care, and a great big hug anytime you need it. This invitation non transferable, it cannot be used by anyone else. Only the touch of your hand is required.

A Good Recipe!

We take a little bit of you and a little bit of me and we blend very carefully. We add smiles, hugs, a taste of laughter, and a large dose of blessings from GOD. We will need a big spoonful of understanding and healthy cup of passion. Just like all good recipes this relationship will also need time. Sometimes you might want to add a little family for spice. It's nice to have your loved ones support. And for that bold flavor we put in just a touch of romance to make it just a little spicy. Oh yeah, this is going to be really good when it's ready. Now we add a few long walks and maybe a picnic or two and some movies are always good. Now we have something special, something that goes beyond conventional relationships. This is a love filled with all the wonder, contentment and peace that we could possibly imagine. We take this incredible mixture and serve with care; this is what a beautiful family is made of. I love you so very much.

A Whole Lot of Fun

We have finally come to the point where we realize that it's all about love. It would be so great if everybody could come to this conclusion. We have come so far in such a short amount of time. The level of trust has reached a point where we no longer question each other's motives. Finally, an atmosphere conducive to true love exists and our union can flourish. To truly become the element of life and passion it is meant to be. Deep down inside the feeling grows and grows until sometimes it can actually scare us. The past experiences can make things difficult when we dwell on them too long. But when we search our hearts we find each other. The warmth and security will never leave, the love will never diminish and I will always be there for you. This is what love should be, overwhelming, all consuming and a whole lot of fun.

Absolutely Nothing!

When everything is quiet and life slows down, and you close your eyes to the rest of the world. I often find myself searching my mind for the right thing to say, looking for the perfect expression of love. With the peace of the moment I come to realize that the perfect thing to say is absolutely nothing.…………………………………………………

Achieving Perfection

There comes a time when a man doesn't want to pretend any more. He doesn't want to play games or even indulge himself in the chase. He starts to realize what real beauty is. I guess I had to grow up at some point in time. The things that make a real difference are not just on the surface; you may have to dig a little to find what you're looking for. It has been so long since I've felt real love that I almost was unable to trust it when it finally came my way. My faith in this matter could not be in the individual but in the INFINITE. My love for you is so strong that I went to my GOD for the answers and HE gave them to me. In you I have found everything that I have been looking for my whole life. The love, the passion, the caring, the nobility, the beauty and most importantly, the faith. I could not love you more because you are everything that I asked for. Waiting all this time is nothing when you achieve perfection. All you have to do is be you to be everything to me.

Apology

This morning I found myself apologizing to GOD because HE was not the first thing on my mind. Normally I'm so grateful just to wake up in good health with another chance to get it right. Everybody doesn't get another chance in this world. It took a long time for me to realize that HE is crazy about me. But on this morning something else occupied my thoughts. Something warm and wonderful, something that made me think of every love song ever written, every love story ever told. It consumed my mind and filled me with an emotion that I thought I was too old to experience. It was you. This beautiful but gentle, wise and incredible woman had come into my life and made it complete. You are the living proof that GOD is crazy about me and only wants the best for me. I can only hope that HE can forgive me for my actions and my thoughts, but with this wonderful gift in place I'm sure HE understands.

At The Movies

Fantasy and imagination go hand in hand when we speak of the things that we wish for. At the movies, often times we see things that we want to be a part of our lives. The tender moments of a love scene seems to bring about wishful thinking, sometimes the scene makes us think of the way we want things to be. With this love I don't have to imagine. The reality of it is that all my dreams, my fantasies, come true every time I see you. There is nothing on the screen that comes close to what we share; no scene in a screenplay that can compare to the passion that dwells within our souls. You have created in me one of the most intense and caring emotional states that I have ever experienced. It's like an adventure through uncharted territories of my heart, finding lost places like Love Island and taking journeys to passion. With you love doesn't just exist, it unfolds.

Bad Dream

This morning I woke up with the most terrible dream in my head. I normally don't remember much about my dreams but this one was so disturbing that it stayed on my mind. In the dream, you were leaving me, just that and that alone. It was the source of so much pain and confusion that I could not take it. Fear is not a normal part of my character but this; this made me feel as if I had no backbone. The thought of loosing you is so scary, as if I would be loosing my whole world. But then I woke up, saw you and realized my world was still complete. I never want to take you or our relationship for granted. The thought of living without your love is unthinkable. If you knew how much I love you, how much I depend on your love. Every moment without you makes me want you even more. I'm so glad that the dream is just a dream and my reality is filled with the presence of you.

Born To Love You

We carry so much inside of us. There is so much accumulated knowledge, experiences, joys and pains. These things mold and shape us into what we are. It can be hard to understand GOD'S plan and the way life is challenging us. With all the things that happen in our lives, I'm so glad that you were made for me. Everything about you is as if you were made for me. I will help you through the hard times and help you celebrate the good. I was born to love you.

Celebrations

Celebrations are always nice to look forward to. I like to see you go through so much fuss about your hair and nails, to be so meticulous about the perfect outfit. The right bag and of course the shoes have to match perfectly. When I go out with you, you make me look good. But the reason for the event can sometimes be bitter sweet. The circumstances that bring us together can reflect a time when events were much more extreme, giving this moment an importance it would not normally have. Regardless of what we celebrate the real fun is just being with you. Celebrating our love is every day, and no special event could take the place of that. The moment that I opened the door for you and saw that smile and that dress, I knew that no matter what, my celebration was complete.

Certain Type of Strength

When I search my heart and
soul for answers about life and love, it seems
that I never really get any definitive results. There are so
many variables in this life experience that influence the outcome
of any given situation that putting them all into perspective can be
mind-boggling. The one thing that I am absolutely sure about is my love and
fascination for you. There is no pretending, no second-guessing, no uncertainty
about you or what I feel for you. There is a certain type of strength that comes from
knowing where your true source of love comes from. When the INFINITE put us together
my level of contentment became unmatched, a feeling of nobility overcame me and the peace
that only comes from real love had finally become my own. Of all the things to be grateful for,
you are the one thing in my life that I am thankful for the most.

Creatures of Habit

By nature we are all creatures of habit. Anything that we do the same way two or three times we will probably continue to do the same way over and over again. Learning to use this aspect of our nature to our advantage can be beneficial. We get up at a certain time and go through our normal ritual to get to our destinations on time. We are even kept on schedule by our pets when they get hungry, always at the same time every day. The habits that I enjoy the most are the ones that bring me closer to you. Every time I see you I get the biggest smile and a kiss from you. Always a warm hug and you always say, hey honey! When I get off from work there is no other thought than simply getting home to you. It's like being on automatic pilot to your house. These are good habits and I'm glade I don't have to break any of them.

Dance of the Leaves

It was on a bright fall day. I was out walking my dog and the wind was blowing and the colors were so bright that the trees looked like they were on fire. It is so cool to see the changing of the seasons. With a strong gust the leaves of a large tree began to fall. Each individual leaf had its own pattern of flight, its own dance. This incredible sight made me realize that the individual dance of the leaves is as unique as one persons love for another. None of us are the same. We all have our own way of doing things, our own way of loving, our own way of dancing. I know that I have never felt this way before, so different, so unique, so much passion and love. My love for you has its own dance.

Elegant Beauty

When it comes to approaching females, I'd like to think that if one is honest enough the task should not be complicated. After all, we are the same, human beings trying to make their way in this great big world. The situation can be made to seem difficult when we look at societies ever changing conditions and rules. I didn't want to play, I didn't want to pretend, and I did not want to loose in my efforts to make you mine. Only the most real forms of communication, and most sincere form of prayer could have brought me to this most amazing point in my life. With a very special love that feels heaven sent, I come to know the elegant beauty and passion that is you. What you bring to me I could never do without.

Eternal Night

There is something special about the culmination of you, the night and your voice. At times it almost seems unreal, the effect that it has on my senses and the amazing emotional content that it contains. This is something that I do not want to live without. Where did you come from? How did you capture my heart? Why does your smile mean so much to me? During the day, when I'm away, my body aches for your touch, the thought of you brings such sweet memories, I can hear you, I can smell you, and I can feel you. There is something about you that makes my past seem as if I have just been pretending. Real joy can be so hard to find. I'm just so grateful that GOD brought me to you.

Fairytales

We tell stories to our children about knights in shining armor, beautiful princesses in the most exquisite gowns waiting to be rescued, noble princes who are all alone in the world until they find the damsel in distress to rescue from things like dragons and evil witches and even stepmothers. These stories always have pleasant endings; ending in happily ever after. But when our youth get older they find life to be totally different. Relationships are not so easy and society has place pressures on them that they could never have anticipated. We find ourselves losing faith in the stories, in ourselves, and at some point even in our GOD. When faith is placed in the right perspective and we realize that love is real, life takes on a whole new meaning. Fairytales are not reality, and life is much more different than the picture that we paint for our children. But perhaps I have found an exception to the rule. I have found something with the grace of the INFINATE that makes the story come true for me. You came into my life and made a fairytale become reality, all the love, passion, support and beauty that one man can imagine. Maybe the stories are not as far off as they seem.

Family

I have heard that youth is wasted on the young. To see a 3-6 year old run and play makes you wonder where all that energy comes from. A child's birthday party can be one of the most impressive displays of youth, wisdom and love. To see a grandfather watching everything quietly as the children play, which is so cool, parents making sure everything is just right from food preparation to child safety to making sure there are no stains on the rug, grownups playing childhood games having so much fun. These things are family, they are love, and they help make us what we are. To share such a special time is truly remarkable. I see the love in your family and in you. I watch your face as a child receives a present. To know that these simple pleasures bring you joy is all I need to find peace for the moment. That's what it's all about; the one that I am in love with finds happiness with her family and with me. What could be more important than that? I will always treat your family like it is my family. That's how much I love you.

Fantasy Come True

There is something about your scent that goes past my conscious thought that is almost primal. It stimulates my senses like nothing else. Then I look at you and find something so alluring that I cannot resist. Your touch gives me pleasures that can only be described as ecstasy. Your warmth takes the entire experience to new heights that I have only dreamed of. When I look into your eyes they tell me so many things but most importantly they tell me that I'm at home. The soft and gentle sound of your voice gives me the satisfaction of knowing that everything is right where it is suppose to be. Now I know what it's like to have my fantasy come true. To be in love and have that love returned.

Fascination With Flight

I have always had a healthy fascination with flight and the way that
it is achieved. Even the Greek myth with Icarus flying to close to
the sun and melting the wax that held his feathers in place kept
my attention for long periods of time. To simply reach out and
find yourself soaring, to climb a thermal like an eagle and
find yourself in a space where no one could follow. Until
the MASTER calls me I'll have to wait for my wings, but
flying is not something that I have to wait for. With a very
special love that only comes from you, I have learned to
take flight and travel to places that were beyond my
imagination. To feel so free that only the air and the
wind could share my experience. You have to be
a very unique and special individual to make
a man feel this way. You have the rare
ability to give my heart wings.

Finding New Worlds

Never be afraid of the man that I am. The things that I do or say are never designed to hurt or tease you. Understanding the love between us is simple but it's not easy. When something as special as this love comes into two people's lives, hearts beat strong, passion rises, emotions take hold and it seems like all the beauty is ever present for all to see. But only we see the awesome colors and the delicate textures of the moment simply because of love. The special times that we share mean so much to me. I always get excited when I anticipate spending time with you. There is a special world that exists and we are the only ones that can see it. Filled with wonder and passion and I'm so glad that I've found this world with you.

Fumbling Through!

The last thing that I want to do is make anything difficult for you when love is suppose to be so easy. I seem to fumble through when I really care about someone and I really care about you. So I ask that you forgive the mistakes that I make and there may be plenty of them. We can do some crazy things when love is involved. It can be hard to think, hard to talk and even harder to act. The elements that make a positive difference in our lives are very seldom easy to gain access to. You have been such a remarkable blessing in my life that sometimes I can't even function properly. The effect that you have on me goes past conscious thought, past any love I have experienced before, beyond the limitations of my heart. Words can no longer express what I feel for you. You have become the most important person on the planet to me. My heart aches for you.

Gentle Touch

We have come so far in such a short period of time. It seems like just yesterday when I first met you, but at the same time it seems like we've been together forever. It's hard to imagine a time before you or a time without you. Who would have thought that this lovely creature is as beautiful inside as she is outside? I take no credit for the success of this relationship. That belongs to the INFINITE and you. With a warm and tender smile you give me strength. With a gentle touch you make me feel so secure. You have taught me that the most difficult battle can be won with faith, love and patience. Just to know what you expect of me makes a difference in my day simply because I love you so much that I don't want to disappoint you. You give me a purpose, a reason to live, to succeed. I want our lives to be filled with all the wonder and love that the world has to offer. With you by my side I believe anything is possible. Just hold on to me and I'll hold on to you. I will never let you go.

Hand In Hand

Yesterday I walked with you and you reached for my hand. It is so good to know that someone needs to be near me as much as I need to be near them. Do you feel the need in me? Do you have any idea of how strong it is? Just to hold your hand means so much to me. Warm and soft to the touch, gentle and ever so graceful, you make walking seem like floating on air. When I walk with you hand in hand the others around us don't even exist, and it seems like all is right with the world. Love is good.

Happy

There are very few things in this life that have the capability to make us truly happy. When we were children, our favorite toy at Christmas time served the purpose. When we were teenagers a driver's license or our first car got us exited. When the summertime came getting out of school filled us with anticipation. Now that we are grown we look forward to vacations and seeing new places. When I think of what I have with you, all of these feelings come to bear. I can't wait get on the road and see you anytime I get the chance. When I get to your door I feel like a kid at Christmas time. The intimate times are always filled with anticipation. There is absolutely nothing that compares to an evening with you. This is what I have dreamed of all my life. To find that special person that makes me feel like I can do anything with you by my side. I adore you little girl!

Holiday with You

Holidays can be a very special time for family and friends. When people come together in love the outcome is always positive. The 4th of July is very different from most holidays in that the celebration is different in each family. Some travel great distances, many wait until it gets dark to light fireworks for the children. They always enjoy the bright lights. You know we like to bar-b-q. The biggest thrill for me was to share the experience of family and friends with you. I love having you by my side, I love laughing with you and sharing the good times. My friends think you are incredible and are so happy for me. You make me look good. With all that you have given me, how could I ever begin to reciprocate? I will give you everything in my heart. All of my dreams, all of my futures, all of my forevers belong to you. I love spending any holiday with you. Just being with you to watch the children play is a special treat. To see you smile at their playing gives me real satisfaction. There is so much that goes on between us that all I can say is, I love you so very much.

How Could I Ever Leave You?

When love is real we may find ourselves doing things that we might not even have considered in the past. To make sacrifices or to extent courtesies or to take the extra step just to see that special person smile. You have done things so far out of the ordinary that it caught me totally by surprise. You made sure that the situation was secure and my act was tight. So much more than words can say, your actions simply speak so clearly. And what you have to say carries such a large degree of importance and love. If there ever is any doubt, just look at what we do when we don't have to do anything at all. You will find that our actions speak of love, our words of passion, and our feelings run much deeper that either one of us could have imagined. How could I ever leave you?

How Could I Possibly Ask For More?

How does one even try to express his true feelings for the woman he loves? Society has placed so many restrictions on emotion that just sorting through the details can become so time consuming. With the presence of you in my life it has become easy and somewhat necessary to let you know how I really feel. The thought of you is constantly on my mind. When I look at you I see the most lovely and pleasant woman, filled with love and virtue. The softest touch and the sweetest scents create the most incredible experiences of passion and love. When you smile at me the feeling of euphoria overwhelms my soul and all I want to do is hold you forever and ever. If I don't get to see you soon I feel like I'm going to explode. You give me the sweetest days and the most sensuous nights. How could I possibly ask for more?

I Am a Believer

I have wanted true for so long that it seemed like it might not ever come to me. I had tried to make the adjustment to being alone, possibly for the rest of my life. All I wanted was the one, you know, the one that was meant just for me. The frustration became overwhelming and I felt so all alone. I prayed every day for that special person to come into my life, someone who would make my world complete. Then, you finally came and changed everything. I mean everything is different now, from the way I think to the way I act and even the way I love. Now I am a believer, in love, passion, beauty and even romance. You have the most amazing way of touching my heart. You do it with peace, understanding, love and patience. So totally unique in your presence, I cannot resist you. And why should I? After all, this is what I prayed for. My GOD is so complete in everything that he does, that when it came to you I should have known that you would be perfect in every way. He made you so loving and stunning, graceful and beautiful. I couldn't help but love you.

I Belong to You

Sometime it seems like all the odds are against us when we look at our friends, our family and even the economy. The day can seem so long when you hear so many negative things about relationships and the things people do to each other in the name of love. It is so refreshing when you look at what we have and come to realize that we do not fit any stereotype that exist. We have a very special love that goes past conscious thought and manifest itself in the sensuous passion that only the two of us share. No one could ever presume to know what exist between us because while it is consistent it is still so dynamic that we are actually amazed at our own actions at times. This love is so good, so soothing, and most important, you belong to me, and I belong to you. We belong to each other. Nothing could possibly come between us.

I saw you

I saw you talking with my friends. Some people who are important to me. With a gentle manor and ease you captured them not unlike the way you captured me. You took time to listen; your response was just enough to maintain their interest but not enough to provoke any negative responses. Balanced with a degree of care and patience that is so unique to you and you alone that I cannot help but be impressed. The way you handle yourself and others is amazing. The way you handle me is incredible. I cannot help but love you, and I do, more than you will ever know. You make me look good.

In My Arms

What does it take to give a man a sense of purpose? What really makes a difference in the life of any individual who craves the touch of that special someone? Predicting what gives a man the things that he needs to be satisfied can be difficult at best. As for me, it's easy to see that you are all I need. I look at you and all the things that a man could hope for simply come to be. With you I have found heaven on earth, a GOD given paradise. I cannot wait to hold you in my arms again and again and again.

In The Meadow

Have you ever been to a meadow in the country, where the birds were chirping and the grass was green and lush, soft supple flowers and maybe a brook running through? You can hear the sound of insects and possibly a path where rabbits run every day, a few large trees with shade enough to sit and enjoy the moment. Life is present and thriving. Well, if it doesn't rain, it's as if life ceases. The grass turns brown and the flowers become brittle. The sounds of life stop and the land seems harsh and barren. Even the trees don't seem the same. But ultimately the rain does come, and almost overnight the meadow is transformed. The grass is green again and the flowers show their true colors in all their glory. The birds return and the bees begin to pollinate. The entire area is alive again. Well.... the way that the meadow needs the rain, that's the way I need you.

In the morning!

One morning I woke up early just to see your face. For some reason it just captured my attention. You looked so peaceful, so content. I wonder if you're dreaming, if it's pleasant, if it's about me. I just enjoy seeing your face in the morning sun. To know that the person that means so much to me is at peace even if only for the moment. Sometimes while you sleep you reach for me, turn to me and hold me as if even in your dreams you still find comfort in my touch. There is so much that goes on in your silence.

Incomplete

I have come to realize that the way I really feel about you is difficult and even impossible at times to describe or share. If you could come inside to see what I see and feel what I feel it would make things so much easier to understand. But nothing worthwhile is ever easy. So I try to show you and tell you what's inside my heart for you. It just never seems to be enough. Maybe that's the way it's suppose to be, maybe I'm suppose to spend the rest of my life showing you how much I adore you. I cannot think of anything else I'd rather do. My life would be incomplete without you.

Just For You

Sometimes we would like to think that we are so complicated. We would even believe ourselves to be so much more than we really are. The fact of the matter is that we are simple creatures. Sometimes we are very sensitive but still it shouldn't be so hard to understand us. There are things that change our attitudes during the course of a day. Displaced hostility can be the result of such changes. We can take out our frustrations on the ones we love the most. These elements of our emotions can be the most difficult to understand. We have come so far in our levels of understanding but the unknown in ourselves can still be a major hindrance in our emotional development. The truth is what we run from and the truth is what we have been looking for the entire time. When you really come to understand what is inside me, you will find that I truly love you and all that you are. This is something that is easy to understand. My love for you is just for you.

Just Plane Old Love

Love in its purest form is the most intimate, passionate and satisfying emotion that anyone could ever experience. It is filled with so much wonder that if I could describe it, the true meaning of the word would be diminished. This simple emotion has the ability to inspire great works, to change the course of events, to build great structures, or to simply warm a cold heart. Used improperly it can be extremely devastating, bringing destruction and despair to unsuspecting individuals. The real secret to true love is to come to realize who really loves you. To find someone who wants you to succeed, to make your program work, someone who wants to see you look good and be supportive of your efforts. I have found such a love, and I will do anything to keep it. No matter what is said or done, this love is the most important personal relationship in my life and you will always be able to depend on my love and support. Just plain old love!

Keys to My Heart

It can be so interesting to see the world through your eyes. When I see you marvel at the graceful flight of a crane on the lake, or the smile that comes to your face when you see a baby. Some of the most simple things make the biggest differences in our lives. You have taught me to look at the world from a fresh perspective. To experience life without preconceived notions and open yourself to all the beauty that the world has to offer. You have taken the keys to my heart and opened it to so much love that I cannot help but love you totally, completely and unconditionally. I can't wait to get home to you.

Learning to trust!

Falling in love can be difficult at best because of the things that we go through in personal relationships and the experiences we have with our loved ones. Learning to trust does not come easy. When you do decide to take a chance it's clouded with the possibility of dishonesty and pain. We will change this mindset. We can make a difference in the way love is perceived. In you I have been given a most precious gift, something that fills my days with the most pleasant thoughts and my nights with the most amazing love. I cannot change the past, but I can make sure that your future has the kind of care that you so richly deserve. I love you, and I will always be very good to you.

Like A Fire Burning

I don't think anyone truly has all the answers to love. Man has sought to understand women and love since the dawn of time. So many books, poems and songs have been written on the subject that we could never experience them all in one lifetime. The insight that anyone has on love comes from ones own experiences and learning. Hopefully, I have been a true student of the art form and can express real love and share as well. We grow in love. For some it can be an endless unfoldment. To come to understand real human emotion can be difficult at best. You have given me a different kind of education on the subject. With patience, understanding, warmth and most of all love, you have taught me that the possibilities are endless, that hope is alive and that love is real. To find yourself in the middle of passion and learn that real love will not abandon you can be the most uplifting feeling, like a fire burning, if you allow it, can consume all that you are. Trust me, this love is yours.

Love Songs

When things haven't gone right in your love life, little things can be a major distraction. To detect scents that are familiar, places the two of you used to go, even seeing someone with the same hair cut can take you back in time and remind you of how it used to be. Love songs are the worst. They bring emotions to the forefront that you've been trying to get away from for a long time. It never seems to really work. The harder you try, the more present the memories seem to be. The way music weaves melodies and harmonies together and when the lyric has been put together just right, it can make the love you lost come rushing in on you. I have found something so special in my life that it gives me the ability to really enjoy a good love song. The love that you give makes every love song that I hear a wonder to behold. Your smile, your touch, seems to create compositions in my head that fill my soul with warmth and compassion. Scripture states that a man who finds a woman finds a good thing. I had no idea of just how good you would be.

Magic!

I looked at you last night and it was like magic. All of a sudden I felt as if I could fly. You turned and smiled at me and the rest of the world just seemed to fade away. I love it when your hair is pulled back and I can see your face. What an incredible sight. When you smile at me I feel like I'm king of the world. I often wonder if you have this effect on others. If I could change anything about you, I wouldn't. If you're not perfect, you are perfect to me. This is the masterpiece, this is the greatest symphony, and this is the greatest love I have ever known. Thank you for being who and what you are to me. You have taught me how to love again, truly love again. Like the breath of life itself it consumes me. Good morning Pooh!

Maybe We Could Take a Walk

Hello! I know that it seems like an old line but you look so familiar. I wonder have we met? In any case I really wanted to meet you. I didn't know how or even if I should, but I really wanted to. You probably get this all the time but I think you are extremely attractive. You must have a host of guys chasing you. I'm just am ordinary guy but I am drawn to you in the most amazing way. I have so many questions like are you from here, what does it take to make you smile, do you like trombones. Kind of crazy huh? If you are as beautiful inside as you are outside I just have to know you. Maybe we could take a walk, or you might like to see a movie or even go kite flying with me. Maybe I'm grasping at straws but I just want to spend some time with you. You are so adorable. If you get tired of your current situation or you feel you just want an effective change or if you just want to be pampered for a while, don't hesitate to come to me. I would love to be there for you.

Morning Glory

The morning is a very special time of day. With the breaking of the dawn's early light, the whole world gets another chance at life and at getting it right. With dew on the grass and the air so fresh, it feels like everything is reborn. Scripture states that even our LORD JESUS got up early in the morning to pray. If you catch it at the right time, you can see at first light the most beautiful flowers bloom. The morning glory only opens at the beginning of a new day. The timing has to be just right, but it is the most amazing sight to see. Your love is almost the same way. Under the right conditions this magnificent transformation happens and a love opens up with such a presence that one cannot help be stunned by the moment. The experience is so consuming that it becomes almost impossible to let go of the feeling. The morning is a very good time for love.

My Heart Belongs to you

These days life can be so uncertain. There are so few things that we can be sure of. There are however three things you can depend on. The first is the HOLY SPIRIT, ever lasting to everlasting, the second is change, no matter what the situation is, it will change in time. The last is our love. No matter what's going on I want you to be secure in knowing when you come to me there will always be the same warm smile, the same safe hug, the same feeling of security that you felt yesterday, and last week, and last month. To know that it will be there tomorrow, and next week, and next month, and forever. You don't have to wake up; it's not a dream. This man is really in love with you. My soul belongs to GOD, but my heart belongs to you.

My Imperfection

Making mistakes is a part of life's imperfection. Add to that the fact that I am male and it becomes even more prevalent. The one thing that I know I did right was to actively seek your love. Of all the things that are dear to me you are by far the most. On this journey we have decided to take please remember that I may trip up sometimes, I may even stumble and fall. But with you by my side I will always get back up and I will never give up. This love, this relationship, this spirit is far too important to me and I will always treat it as a gift from GOD. Your love is so necessary for me to find my way. Forgive me for the changes that I may put you through and remember you are the most important human on the planet to me. All my love!

Never Disappointed!

The things that shape our character, the experiences that make us what we are can give us the ability to protect our hearts from the things that would harm us. These defense mechanisms can be very beneficial to us when dealing with the rebel element. But when the right person final comes along these same defense measures can hamper the true relationship we are supposed to have. I know how you feel because I have the same feelings. Haven't you noticed that we share the same emotional ties? I feel what you feel. In actuality this is the blessing. How amazing is it that we share the same emotional content that at times we can even be of the same mind. When we learn to trust this amazing connection we will become so strong that with GODS grace nothing can withstand us. When I come near you I feel things that I cannot explain. This euphoria is overwhelming. It becomes all that I am. When I let it take control with the combination of you, I am never disappointed. I tell you these things because I am trying to describe the love I feel for you and how much you mean to me. Never be afraid, my love is never designed to hurt or tease you.

Nothing Compares to You

Everything is not always black and white. There are many different shades of gray, especially when it comes to people. We come in so many wonderful hues and colors, that's what makes the world so beautiful. Anything less would make life so boring. I held your hand up in the sunlight and beheld the contrast and the beauty of it all. Your skin is fresh and your hand so warm and comfortable. The color of your skin against mine is such a lovely sight. It reminds me of just how different we really are and still have so much in common. The differences allow us to explore elements of each other and the things we have in common let us come together in so many special ways. This is a very special love. So unique that I often find myself daydreaming about you and what your doing, reminiscing about the night before and the day to come. I don't have anything to compare you to because there is nothing that compares to you. Whatever it is that you have makes me long for you every second that we are apart.

Out of My Element

When you take anything out of its element the results are always awkward and can be dangerous. A fish out of water to long will perish; an eagle with the tips of his feathers clipped cannot fly. Bound to the ground it cannot feed its young. A country and western musician is totally lost on stage with a jazz band and vice versa. Often times I feel out of place when I try to express my true feelings for you. Writing is not something that I practice a lot of, especially when you talk about a letter of love. So if it seems that the things that I say may seem a little out of place please forgive me. But when the love comes rushing in it can be hard to contain. One finds himself needing to express what's inside, to explore new ways opening ones heart and soul. So I put pen to paper and try to achieve a level of understand that is conducive to real togetherness. My success in this matter is purely because of the way you make me feel. I cannot take credit for the type of emotion that you have rising within me. The inspiration that you provide lifts my spirit and gives me the frame of mind to truly be able to love. For this I am ever so grateful.

Pain!

To look at ones life fully, the aspect of pain has to be examined. Always carrying a negative connotation, it represents some of the darkest aspects of our personalities. In reality, pain shapes our character; it teaches us about the things we do not want to experience again. It brings a unique understanding of the kind of people and events that are detrimental to our lives. One of the biggest problems is that when we experience pain for long periods of time it can distort our perception of relationships and our own emotions. When the right person comes along to give us true love we don't understand it, we mistreat it, and sometimes we even reject it. In short, it blocks our blessings. When we open ourselves to the total experience of life we find that pain can be a very important tool. Keeping us safe from harm, and guiding us away from the things that challenge a positive emotional state. In showing us what we do not want, it shows what we do want. My pain has brought me to this point in time. It has taught me about what I want definitively, and what I want is you. A beautiful woman with extreme sensitivity, a gentle touch with a strong hand. A woman with powerful faith, and wisdom, and a woman who smiles at me and melts my heart, a woman that loves life as much as I do, and a woman that loves me and wants the best for me. Pain is an incredible teacher and you are a wonderful lover. I accept all the pain in my life and do gladly as long as it means I can have you.

Part of My Soul

Being the man that I am, sometimes I feel that you deserve something special, something that is all for you, something that only you can claim. What could be unique to you and you alone? Something that expresses love, patience, understand and beauty. I think I'll write a love song. A song that is easy and flowing. Pleasing to the senses and challenging to the ear, a song that gives the most beautiful image of the night, you, and love, a song written just for you, a simple melody that only we can share. But to me it sounds like orchestral perfection. In this way I can give you something that can only come from me. This is my most pure expression of love. With all that you have given me, this gift gives you a part of my soul.

Part of the Human Condition

I ask myself just how this love came to be. Something so special that has been molded by the longing of two hearts, with fate being so generous to us. For a long time we suffered from relationships that simply were not meant to be. For lack of a better way of saying it, the games that people play are played way too much. We all must come to understand that making mistakes is a very important learning tool. It is simply a part of the human condition. It is never wrong for you to be who and what you are. That is what makes you so special, and you are definitely special to me. With all the imperfections that exist within us, just the chance to get it wrong or right is still truly a blessing. When it comes to you, I am lost in a world of unimaginable pleasures. A place where passion is an everyday occurrence, understanding is the key to a peaceful existence, and love is the foundation on which we stand.

Peace and Love

When I started my day I did everything just like the day before. The normal routine gets me out of the door on time. For some reason I started missing you. Pretty pictures of you started appearing in my mind and my heart got so heavy, it felt as if I had not seen you in forever, but we were together just yesterday. Everything that I remember about you, the way you sound, the way you smell, the way you taste, even the way you feel became real to me even though you weren't there. You have become so much a part of me that you may have become the largest part of my reasoning and my thoughts. As the day begins and my responsibilities present themselves my memories of you put me at ease and I can approach each situation with a certain calmness and peace. You give me so much but the most important thing you give is the peace and love we share.

Pretty Feet

An old friend who I highly respect told me one day that he loved a woman with pretty feet. When I asked him why he replied, if she takes care of her feet she takes care of everything else. I have seen the way you take care of your family, the way you take care of your responsibilities, and the way you take care of your friends. With a warm and loving hand you handle the most delicate situations with diplomacy and tact. The way you handle me.......well, let's just say that I'm very happy man. And oh yes, you do have extremely pretty feet. Love you Pooh.

Putting the Day Aside

Let's put the day aside. We can do something totally different from our normal routine. Maybe you could show me how to dance or I could show you how to play a song on the piano. Perhaps we could go to the lake just to watch the ducks play in the water. If we get away from the daily grind, instead of concentrating on work or responsibility, we can focus on each other. I want to feel what I feel when all that is on my mind is you. I know that it's selfish but there comes a time when we need to share our love without anything or anyone else getting in the way. I want to hold your hand and walk for a while. I want to feel the sunshine on my face while I watch you try to catch a fish. It might sound strange that something so simple could mean so much to me. When it comes to you, it has never taken a lot to make me content, just your presence is enough to satisfy me.

Real Passion

When I think about all the things that make a difference in our lives, and yes I mean our lives, passion comes to mind more than anything else. What we share is so unique and so rare. My heart races at the thought of you. All the images in my mind are so clear and vivid of you. It seems that all that I am is consumed by your love. I get frantic and excited at the simple mere thought of you. As of right now, I cannot express my true feelings because they are so strong I just don't know how. I'm waiting for you to come, and I will wait as long as t takes. Feel what I'm feeling. Understand the intensity. My GOD, what has happened for me to come to this? I....love you......so very much.

Replacing You Is Unthinkable

I watched a flock of geese as they carried out their daily routine. Searching for food, grooming themselves, playing in the water. Isn't it so cool how they fly in formation? I find it fascinating to see how protective they are of their young. There was one individual, all alone. Somehow his mate had been lost, part of a larger family but still alone. Many species of animals mate for life including geese. It was a little sad to see anything seem so lonely. All I ever wanted was you. I think that I understand the logic behind the life partnership now. If I lost you I would be so lost, so devastated. Replacing you is unthinkable; living without you is beyond my comprehension. When real love is in your life, there is no substitute for it. There is no substitute for you. This life, our relationship is a very precious gift, to be protected and nurtured. For me, living without your love is not an option; it is a very necessary part of my existence.

Road Rage

I got off from work and all I could think about was getting home as fast as I could just to see you. I found myself developing road rage at the five o'clock traffic. Why do people take stupid pills just before they get on the road when I'm trying to get to the woman I love? Then I realized that you love me too and everything would be all right. The pleasant thoughts came into my mind and visions of you put me at ease. It's funny how a simple thought can change the entire moment and make something difficult seem so easy. When I think of love I think of you. When I think of real joy, peace, and contentment I think of you. I can't seem to get you off my mind. When I finally get across town and make it to my final destination I find you there waiting patiently. Real peace is hard to come by. I'm so glad that peace and the thought of you go together. Nothing could ever take your place.

Serenity

There are so many things that challenge us on a daily basis, everything from being at work on time to the opinions of others. Let's face it, finances could always be improved. It just seems that so many things are present attempting to make us feel less than what we are. The spirit that dwells within me enables me to be strong enough to address the issues of this incredible gift of life. The things that are most important to me are the things that occupy my thoughts the most. My days are filled with pleasant thoughts and my nights are filled with the sweetest dreams of you. The presence of you is one of the most powerful gifts I could ever receive. What you give me could never be replaced. Nothing could make any of my days bad because I know that GOD has to be crazy about me to give me anything as special as you. Somehow you fill my mind with serenity and a peace that I have never known before. Life's challenges seem so small compared to your love.

Showing Out!

Their came a time in my life of great uncertainty, a time when my path was not so clear and I found myself stumbling along the way. It can be so confusing when you don't take time to listen to GOD. Then I came to realize just how important you are in my life. The MASTER placed you here, brought us together for so many fantastic reasons, but the one that is most important to me right now is the simple fact that in my short comings, only a precious gift like you could give me the support I need to move forward. With all the things that you are, the beauty, the passion, the gracefulness, the gentle touch, your insight, faith, and love help to fortify my life. When the INFINATE made you he was showing out.

Simple Pleasures

When things finally begin to slow down and we start to fell at ease, there is a very different way of communicating that takes place between us. Your voice becomes soft and sweet. A mere whisper from you is as effective as shouting it from a rooftop. The ever so soft sound of you gives me delight and warmth. It is so easy to get lost in the moment when the gentle sound of your voice with just a subtle hint of a southern accent is heard on a summer evening. When everything is quiet, and the silence is all we hear, every sound you make is like music to my ears. Whenever we take the time for us we always enjoy our love. These are the most precious moments to me, the simple pleasures that make my day worthwhile.

Something Fantastic

Something fantastic happens when a man falls in love with a woman. The sky seems just a bit clearer; the trees seem to be just a little bit greener. You may find yourself enjoying children playing on the playground or maybe just watching a flock of birds take flight and wondering about the beauty and mystery of it all. The most simple things seem to bring a smile to your face. The anticipation of coming together for any reason can make hearts race, plans change, and new possibilities become endless. I know these things to be true because I have fallen in love with you. The changes that are happening I welcome with open arms. There is finally someone in my life more important than myself. I am a much better man since you came into my life and the reality of it is that the thought of you makes me stop and think about any given situation before I act upon it. If it was just me, I might throw caution to the wind, but where you are concerned, I don't take chances, not with the one I love. You are so dear to me.

Support

When everything is going good in your life, the need for someone to lean on doesn't seem so important. The need for support might not even exist. When things are going wrong you may find yourself lost in a world of confusion and despair. At that time we find out who our real friends are, who really cares for us. In my time of disappointment I find you there in the most supportive role of my friend and my lover. What you give cannot be explained or replaced. You make everything so much better with just your presence. I will always be there for you, no matter what. If you don't want someone around for the bad times, why would you need them around for the good? I love you so very much.

Sweet!

If there is anything that gives me the feeling of warmth and contentment it is you. To find myself at peace in the most adverse situations, and to be able to reason when things are at there worst. The thought of you is just so soothing and calm that when things are challenging I can approach it head on because at the end of the day I know that there is a lovely and caring woman that will welcome me with open arms and all the love that I have ever dreamed of. The most amazing blessing, the most amazing love, and the most incredible woman I have ever known. I can only hope that I can give you a portion of what you have given me. Please, stay as sweet as you are.

Thank You

I want to thank you for always taking my feelings into consideration. I realize that it's not easy to balance everything in your life, especially when someone like me has entered the equation. In any case, I will always try to be sensitive to your needs, understanding to your emotional state and supportive of the moves you make. The simplicity of your expressions, the depth of your thoughts makes me realize than I am truly blessed to have you in my life. I hope you never change.

Thank you for the love!

With everything that happens during the course of the day, all the work, the people, the problems, the adversity, it is so nice to simply have the memories of you. Filling my mind with peace and love, giving me the feeling of total contentment. It seems we have come so far in such a short amount of time. How do you do what you do? It cannot be easy dealing with someone like me. With you I have learned that there is nothing as strong as gentleness, nothing as gentle as real strength. I cannot imagine one single day without you. Thank you for the understanding, the chance, the patience, and most of all thank you for the love.

The Angel I Prayed For

Every man has needs. Addressing them at times can be no small task. I have been blessed to have someone like you who comes to understand the unique requirements in my life. What you bring to this relationship is nothing short of amazing. You give me strength when I need it, support in difficult times, understanding when I'm confused, passion and love in the most sensuous moments, and most of all, you give me the reason to dream and work for the dreams fulfillment. With the introduction of you into my life, my most delicate emotional needs are met and the things that might hinder me in the past have been simply put into place. I thank GOD every day for sending me the angel that I prayed for.

The Boat of Captain John

Every now and then we bare witness to some very special days. Early on a Sunday morning when I opened my eyes and realized you were with me I found myself drawn to you. All I wanted to do was please you. In this matter I found myself highly successful. How blessed can two people be just to begin the day with sunshine, love and a prayer. We take time out for our GOD and he continues to bless. After the events of the day we take time for friends and ourselves. We board the boat of Captain John and take to the water. Who knew we needed this time so much. The peace and serenity was totally indescribable. I watched the sun as it shined through your hair as the wind blew through it. To see you smile at that moment in time was all the confirmation that I needed to know you were happy. I need you to understand that this is the most beautiful sight to me. If I could I would give you these experiences every day. I guess that is what makes this day so special, the simple fact that it doesn't happen every day. But please understand that my love for you grows constantly. Thank you for being who and what you are. The woman that makes my heart sing.

The Greatest Education

Sometimes I just don't understand why we are so different or why we seem to be on totally opposite ends of the spectrum when it comes to ideas or even compromise. Could it be that our personalities are that foreign to each other or is it simply because of masculine and feminine attitudes. We can be so far apart at times that it's like we don't know each other. But if you are away from me for more than a day I cannot take it. Being away from you is the most uncomfortable feeling, the longing and the wondering is just too much. I have always heard that I'll know when the right one comes. Well, now I know, without you everything is so incomplete and learning to celebrate our differences is quite possibly the greatest education that I will ever experience. There is no way that I could do without you.

The Scent of You

There is a very special scent that is so light and very distinctive to my senses. I often find myself feeling the air for the source of this aroma. It has become so much a part of my being that to be without it for any period of time means I almost feel lost. It's so delicate and pleasant, but at the same time it has such a strong hold on me. When I come near I find that it's you. I can be anywhere and know if you are in the room or down the hall or even present at all. You are in my system. You are a part of me now; maybe the best part me. The scent brings me to you, and the taste of your skin will not let me leave. Whatever GOD created in you is designed to fill me with the reason to love. Isn't it amazing that something so soft and gentle can bring a man like me to his knees? I cannot get enough of you.

The Soft Touch of Your Skin

I find it difficult to speak on intimate details of our relationship, but I do feel that you need to know what happens when I'm near you. There are times when the soft touch of your skin is all I need to calm my spirit. Looking into your eyes I see the culmination of years of nurturing, loving and learning how to give. The gentle scent of your hair is such a delicate and pleasant aroma. It gives me a very special peace of mind. Your kiss is much more than I could ever describe. When I hold you in my arms it just seems like I cannot get close enough to you. These feelings are made ever present for the simple fact that I am in love with you. Being with you is not an option for me; I need you so very much.

The Ultimate Satisfaction

I watched as you prepared yourself for church. You are quite honestly the most beautiful woman I have ever known. While in front of the mirror I watched you transform yourself from beautiful to absolutely stunning. I'm not sure if I understand whole concept of make up or even if I like it. But I observed you apply a very delicate powder to your face and lipstick is something that I am familiar with. You seem to utilize these things with such a delicate hand. The way you comb and shape your hair is like watching an angel. I saw you pick the perfect set of earrings and a most impressive ornament to adorn your graceful neck. When you turned and faced me I could not believe my eyes. I have always found you incredibly attractive, inside and out, but this moment will stay with me. To see you smile at me and know that you are mine gives me the ultimate satisfaction. You are absolutely adorable.

The Woman That You Are

You don't have to do anything to impress me. No special look, no purchased item, no incredible place to be could make any difference in how I feel about you. If there was ever anything established in my heart, it is my love for you. We are challenged on a daily basis to maintain a certain amount of discipline and love. Just the woman that you are is more than enough to keep this man content. The sheer pleasure, peace and serenity that you bring is something that I could never do without. My senses are always so exited whenever you come near. The sound of your laughter, your scent, your taste, the touch of your skin, the sight of your lovely face, these things transform a normal day into the most phenomenal love experience that one could possibly imagine. Don't worry, as soon as my day is finished, I will be coming strait home to you.

This is your love!

It can be so hard to put things in perspective between two people when your emotions are involved, so many variables to consider, so many memories that you are reminded of, too many opinions. We live in a world of so much uncertainty and we don't have time to waste. But where love is concerned there is one thing you can be sure of, if you loose heart don't worry, I will give you mine. There is something here that is very soft and gentle but at the same time very strong. Make no mistake about it, it is yours. You do not have to share it, worry about it, or go through any changes over it. This is your love!

Time

I feel that too much time is spent worrying about things that we cannot change, don't need to change, don't have the will or the means to change, or simply don't know how to change. Time is wasted on things that don't matter in our lives. Sometimes it feels like we don't have the answers to anything. With all the things that occupy our time, it is such a comfort to know that your love is never a waste of time. When we come together it's always a true expression of love and tenderness, devotion to our GOD and ourselves, understanding of our perspective emotional states, and a respect of this most important relationship. When I come to you I know that true love exist, my love. I claim it with all my heart. Every morning I wake up with you on my mind, all the day is filled with visions of you, when the day is finished, I can't wait to get home because I know that a great big hug and a warm smile is waiting there for me. The best time of my life is whenever I spend time with you.

Too Much Fun

I never could have imagined that the person that has become my best friend could also be the most incredible love I have ever known. I anticipate each moment with you. Your laugh is so cool. We have too much fun when were together. Let's go kite flying the next time we have a good wind. Please come to understand that a broken heart can always mend. As long as I'm alive I will always be your old friend.

Today

In the course of a day so many thoughts of you come and go without ever sharing them with you. So TODAY I will try to give you an idea of what my thoughts are. There is the most beautiful picture of you in my mind. Sometimes I daydream about you and the endless possibilities. I can't wait to take you kite flying, for a walk in the park, a picnic or anything that makes you happy and brings us closer. I want to thank you for reminding me that I can still feel, that I'm still human and can experience real joy. You bring these wonderful things into my life by just being you. No one could ever take your place. I love it when you reach for my hand or just invade my space.

Tonight We're Going Out!

Tonight we're going out. I can't wait to see you when you complete the change from workingwoman to this adorable exquisite creature that I am so proud to call my own. When you walk through that door you make the night complete. To see you come to me and reach for my hand lets me know that I'm never really alone and love is always in my life. You are the most stunning and alluring woman that I have ever known. In that dress you could make a man loose his religion. I'm just glad that we share our faith so I don't have to go through those types of changes. I love having you by my side at all times. When you invade my space I feel so secure and confident because I know that you are with me and me alone. There is no pretending or misunderstanding. Tonight I'm going out with the most beautiful woman who loves me and wants to see me smile. You make me a very happy man.

Total Harmony

Sometimes I think that I am a prisoner of my own imagination. The things that occupy my mind can take me to places so real that it feels like I'm really there. What stays in place most of the time is the thought of you. Visions of places we experience, past present and future, even thinking of the bar-b-q on the 4th of July and how much fun it's going to be. I see you laughing with friends and playing with children and most of all sharing your love with me. You are so easy to love and even easier to imagine you with me in total harmony. The hardest thing to do sometimes is simply to open my eyes and have the daydream end. I miss you.

Treasure

There comes a time at the end of the day that I approach with a great deal of anticipation, a time when things slow down and every thing is quiet. A time when you and I come together just to share each others thoughts and experiences of the day, to touch and be touched, to give support where it is needed, to take time out just to show one another that we care. It doesn't have to be anything special, but it always is. It becomes a unique time of a passionate bonding, not just love, but a blending of our spirits, a joining of our souls that creates something new, a type of growth that makes us stronger whenever we are together. It solidifies our relationship to our GOD and to each other. Sometimes it is a time for prayer, sometimes it's a time for play, and quite often it is a time for love. Of all the things that hold my attention during the course of the day, I treasure this incredible time with you the most.

True Vision of Loveliness

There are times at night when my sleep goes so deep that it allows true imagination to produce visions and dreams that are so vivid that it feels like I can reach out and touch them. I can see the most beautiful pictures of you in so many places, different settings, and vivid colors. They always seem to be in the most pleasant surroundings, with a bright sky, green gardens, and the sweet sounds of nature. I do not retain control of the dream; it just seems to unfold in the most inspiring ways. I have never had a love take effect like this before. Just to have one incredible, intelligent, and loving woman fill my mind with thoughts that simply bring me peace. You are a true vision of loveliness.

Unbalanced!

It's so different to feel the same as the one I love. Normally relationships are unbalanced, and one person feels more than the other. Sometimes that individual feels taken advantage of, or even cheated out of the experience they think they should have. It is so good that we have bypassed all these negative emotions that we can have everything that love has to offer. There is never a time when I second-guess my options with you. I trust that if I make a wrong move the woman I love will take time to remind me of it. She keeps me together, she helps me find the way, she gives me love unconditionally, and she keeps me strong. You complete the man that I am. It seems that when I say I love you it's not enough. The true expression, the passion that I feel for you is more than I could ever have imagined. To know that you could feel the same way melts my heart. I am in love with you and I believe that you feel the same way. I miss you Pooh!

Unconditional Love

I once thought that real love was beyond my reach. After having so many rich experiences I had come to the conclusion that maybe true love, having the one, was something that just was not for me. My life has been filled with some of the most incredible moments. So many things to learn, so many places to go, so many people to meet and so much work to do. It just seemed so incomplete until I met you. Now I see so much clearer, my path is so strait, and my heart is so free. When you came into my life, the changes that took place were so very welcome. With nothing more than the things that you are, you have made the most phenomenal additions to a life that has needed you for so long. Why don't you stay for a while, or maybe even forever. I will show you unconditional love, and unbridled passion.

Warm Fuzzy Feeling

I knew you were coming. I didn't know how, I didn't know when, I didn't even know what you were going to look like. After all the things that have happened, good and bad, I have learned that religion is easy, faith is the hard part. So, I place my faith in the INFINITE, I prayed for a highly intelligent, warm, beautiful, loving and caring woman. I prayed for someone who knows how to love, someone who captivates me and gives me that warm fuzzy feeling. I didn't know it but to receive this blessing I had to go through experiences that would prepare me to love you the way you deserve. After all these things came to pass, you came into my life. I received everything that I prayed for. I could not have asked for more. The most incredible woman has made my life full and complete, as if I'm finding my way out of the dark. No man could love you more.

Watching You

I watch you all the time. I watch you when you cook, when you drive, when you shop, I love to watch you when you walk. I watch every word that comes out of your mouth. I watch your moves when you're on the phone. I even watch the pattern of breathing when you relax. I love to watch you sleep, that is very special to me. I watch you not because of anything other than the simple fact that I am in love with you, and I want to know everything about you so I can please you. You mean the world to me.

What Dreams Are Made Of

There have been so many broken dreams in all our lives that after it happens so many times we stop dreaming altogether. The rebel element tries to keep us of balance, to block the thoughts and state of mind that brings blessings, and brings us closer to GOD. The human mind is so incredible; it can take you places that are so extreme that they could only exist in our imaginations. I cannot and will not stop dreaming. It was because of my dreams that I prayed for you to come into my life, and I got what I prayed for. So you see, I believe in dreams and I won't allow anyone or anything to break them. All of the things that you are make up the sum of my dreams of the perfect love. Kind and gentle, soft to the touch, pleasant to hear, sweet to the taste, warm to my heart. You are truly what dreams are made of.

What I do not like!

I do not like being away from you. I do not like it when we have to leave each other. I do not like it when you say goodbye. I absolutely do not like it when we have to be apart more than a day. Does this mean that I am in love? Am I so far gone that I can't even tell? You are the most amazing woman. Girl, you got it going on like a pot of neck bones, with rice.

What Stevie Wonder Said!

There was a quiet afternoon interrupted by a gentle rain. Something about the sound of the soft, gentle summer rain that creates a feeling of contentment. Every now and then I heard the rumble of thunder in the distance. This is a very peaceful time, a time for reflection, a time for the sweetest thoughts of you. Love is very peaceful, that's what Stevie Wonder said.

When I First Saw Your Face...

When I first saw your face I was totally blown away. All I wanted to do was touch it, to feel the softness of your skin, to gently brush my hand against your brow. With all that you are, your face simply captivated me from the very start. I'm sorry that I had to use one of your friends to get to you but she already new who I was and I couldn't let you get away. There was something special about you from the start that caught my attention and made the night unique. Deep down inside I knew that I could love you forever. It didn't matter if anything else went right or wrong that night. The only thing that mattered was my introduction to you. If I got half the chance I was determined to show you that real love was still possible, that real men do exist, and that there is something special waiting just for you. Every thought, every dream, every expectation about you manifest itself in reality. You are the one that makes my world complete.

With You

When I'm with you the words don't always come out right. They seemed to be mixed with the thrill of the moment along with a high degree of emotion. Please understand that you have the most incredible affect on me. If I could explain it, it would be as if it didn't mean as much. You are truly an amazing woman. I miss you.

Without Any Effort

There are melodies that run through my mind whenever I'm feeling less than my normal self. When I can't put my finger on whatever is bothering me. Songs that are familiar to me yet they seem to be new at the same time. Things go wrong sometimes and the challenges of these rebel elements make us stronger. Within the recesses of my imagination I can visit a place where my heart beats strong and the feeling of control is still my own. I put my trust in the song because it is present and I can hear it so clearly. The problem is that in this beautiful melody I cannot find you. The things that make up the entity that is you are so unique that only your physical presence will suffice. Nothing that exists in my imagination comes close to having the real experience with you. Just to have you near creates songs, portraits, sculptures, and the most incredible works of art without any effort whatsoever. This is the real strength, the real blessing, to be able to bring peace in a chaotic mind and fill my heart with real love.

Wondrous

I have seen some wondrous things in my lifetime. The incredible bloom of a dogwood on an Easter Sunday morning, rainbows that stretch across the open sky, the hatching of an egg, and to see a new baby chick emerge to arise and go forth, things that touch your heart and also challenge your mind. The most amazing thing is that they remind me that there is a GOD. After I came to realize who and what is in control, you came into my life. You changed my life in ways that I could not have imagined. You gave me a love that is so different that it could only be heaven sent. You contain a beauty that is almost angelic. After all the things that I have seen in this life, your love is by far the most wondrous thing that I have ever experienced. Through you the INFINITE has given me peace.

Work of Art

Understanding is such a beautiful thing. Between the two of us it is so present that we sometimes take it for granted. This relationship is like a fine musical instrument. For it to perform properly it needs to be tuned to the individual instruments that are performing with it. Each string must be stretched to the right length; each slide must be pulled out to the proper position. When all the elements are in place the potential of a great performance becomes possible. The same is true with our love. We have tuned into each other in such a way that the performance is astounding. There are times when I'm with you that I hear the sweetest sounds, feel the most pleasant sensations. When we are at our best, and this relationship is tuned just right, we share so many fantastic experiences that it becomes almost unbelievable. I have been truly blessed with your presence and your love. Your delicate expressions of compassion and faith give me real strength and make this love experience a wonderful work of art. You are so special to me.

You Are Everything to Me

When I examine the possibilities of chance in our relationship I wonder just how it all came to be. All the situations and relationships that did happen, the ones that didn't happen and the ones that could have happened. They shaped and molded us into what we are right now. The good and bad times, the pleasures and yes even the pain has given us a unique perspective on life and love. It is so incredible that after all this time the INFINITE would bring us together at this point in our lives. The man that I am could not love you more. I could not need you more. You could not be more beautiful to me. I am so grateful for all the things that have made me what I am so I can be who and what I need to be for you. Like so many intricate pieces of a puzzle, we fit. I cannot help but love everything about you because you were designed just for me. I can only hope that you feel the same way. You are everything to me.

You Are My Family

I have found a new reason to succeed, a reason to excel, a reason to make my dreams come true. There have always been reasons to make my life productive and complete. The love of myself was enough to make me move. The man that I am is of discrete identity. I never needed anyone else to acknowledge that fact. Then you came into my life and changed everything. Now there is someone in my life more important than myself. Your happiness and joy are mine also. The main goal has changed from personal gratification to making you smile. There is nothing more important to me than your well being. I'm not sure how it happened but I'm so glad that it did. Your happiness has become so important to me that nothing else matters when it comes you. You are my family now, and what could be more important than that.

You Are My Rib

It is so nice to have a friend like you, someone who has my best interest at heart. You make sure that I address all problems accordingly, good or bad. You help maintain my spirit; you even try to make sure that I eat properly. You give me love! You have become my best friend in this difficult and trying world, a true blessing to behold. Who would have thought that my best friend would also be my lover? The things that you are make me a better person, a better friend, a better man. You keep me strong in a world that preys on the weak. Just as Adam had Eve, you are my rib.

You Are the Queen

I haven't had the type of support that you give in such a long time. I almost forgot how to share the bad times with anyone else. In a real relationship it can be so important to allow someone to be there for you. With such a delicate touch you give me what I need and supply the type of love that makes a man feel complete. To have such a beautiful face smile at me is more than enough to get me through any given situation. You give my world the queen that it deserves.

You Blow My Mind

I wanted; no I needed to let you know just how beautiful you are to me. Every time I look at you I see the most incredible creature. From the smoothness of your skin to the wonderful way your hair smells to the love I see in your eyes. I love to see you walk particularly when you're walking away, and when you walk toward me I know there is a special greeting just for me. You blow my mind when you put on that dress with those heels. Girl you could almost make a man loose his religion. In a pair of jeans you are most impressive. The way your skin glows in the sunlight lets me know that there is nothing that could compare to your beauty or your love. If there is anything in my life that contains any virtue or worthy of any praise, it is you. I love to hold your hand.

Your love

As I walked down the hall I can smell the scent of candles and you. The light grows dim, and as I enter the room, I can see your unmistakable figure in the mirror. I do so enjoy watching you comb your hair as you prepare it for the evening's activities. This is one of life's simple pleasures. When I touch your skin it feels like fine silk and its sweet taste simply melts my heart. You take my hand, an invitation that I cannot refuse. Nothing compares to your love.

Your Warmth

When I opened my eyes this morning and realized where I was, I reached for you. Your warmth filled my hand and my heart with anticipation. This is where I want to be. This is where I belong. Just before the dawning of the day GOD gives me the most precious gift. With the early morning, the presence of you and a very special love, the start of my day is complete. In time you may come to understand my true feelings for you. Make no mistake about it, you are number one and all that I am is yours. You are every song that I sing, the painter of the colors of my mind. As soon as I leave, I miss you.

Finale

When one embarks on a journey, starts a new project or even begins to create something new, if one is sincere in their efforts, an attempt to be the best is what we find in that individual. There is something in the human blood, in the human spirit that can be so competitive that only ones best will suffice. When you came into my life I found myself reaching deep down inside myself to pull out all the love that GOD has given me. It feels as if only the best, the most honest, sincere and true love would have to be in place for this, the most important woman in my life. There are defense mechanisms in place around the heart that can hamper this process and delay the desired completion of our union. Overcoming them is no small task. Any effort, any sacrifice, any trial or tribulation that I have to go through to secure this love is worth all my heart and soul. You are that important to me. Please come to understand that what you bring to me could never be replaced. A love supreme is what everyone is looking for. In the end the blessing that is you and you alone gives me what I need to be the best me that I can be. I can honestly say without any doubt, I love you, I need you, and I'll always be by your side. I thank the LORD for every

Omega

I never dreamed that we would ever be apart. I never imagined that I could hurt you so deep that you would turn and walk away. When I look at the reasons why, I have to accept the fact that it is all my fault. Everything that I told you, everything that I said is still true and my love for you is stronger than it has ever been. I knew that I was in love with you but I did not know just how much until you were gone. At this point I find it impossible to pick up the pieces of my broken heart. Sometimes I just stare at them and try not to cry. You have been the most wonderful and loving woman that I have ever known. Next to GOD you have been the most important thing in my life even if it did not always seem that way. I am so sorry for the changes that made us grow so far apart. After all the love that we have shared I could never turn my back on you. There are elements in place that try to protect my heart but it is to late for that now, you're gone and I miss you so much. I had written a song a long time ago but the words never really came into focus until now.

I have been right there

Right there until the end

And as long as I'm alive

I will always be your old friend

Please come to understand

A broken heart can always mend

If you could forgive my love

I'd still be there, your old friend

We have come this far by faith

But you just couldn't wait

And now it's just to late

I have been right there

Right there until the end

And as long as I'm alive

I will always be your old friend

The omega of this relationship is not the end of my love for you. There is a very old saying. "When you reach the end of the story, close the book". It has been so hard to let you go but if you must go you can take my love with you. Maybe next lifetime!

Within the recesses of my imagination is a special place, just for you and me. Where strength is gentle, and love is the beginning of life.

Ivan G. Hall

Printed in the United States
By Bookmasters